The Bathroom Trivia Book
Volume 2

FASCINATING FACTS
FOR THE FOREMOST
SEAT OF LEARNING

By

Jack Kreismer

RED-LETTER PRESS, INC.
SADDLE RIVER, NEW JERSEY

First Things First

The Lincoln penny was the first United States coin to have a portrait.

• • • •

The first man to walk in space was Aleksei Leonov, in 1965.

• • • •

President Rutherford B. Hayes owned the first Siamese cat in the United States.

• • • •

Ida M. Fuller of Ludlow, Vermont, was the first person to receive a Social Security payment. She received check number 00-000-001 for $22.54 on January 31, 1940.

• • • •

The Indy 500 was first run in 1911 and today it draws the largest crowd of any single-day sporting event in the world.

• • • •

The first person to have her gall bladder removed in the U.S. was Mary Gartside who went under the knife, July 4, 1885.

• • • •

The first station to play rock 'n roll exclusively was WHB in Kansas City.

• • • •

Sports Illustrated's initial Sportsman of the Year, in 1954, was the world's first sub-four minute miler, Roger Bannister.

• • • •

The first U.S. President born in the twentieth century was John F. Kennedy (1917-1963).

• • • •

"Bob" was the first male name given to an Atlantic hurricane.

Four-letter word department: There are four U.S. Presidents whose last names consisted of only four letters- Bush, Ford, Taft and Polk.

• • • •

Sonny and Cher used to work under the names Caesar and Cleo.

• • • •

If you climbed in the old family car and started driving at 50 miles an hour without stopping, assuming you had a bottomless gas tank (and a bottomless bladder), it would take you about 16 million years to go just one light year. Since it's over 4 light years to the nearest star besides the sun, be sure to pack a lunch!

Privia

In just one day, 6.8 billion gallons of water are used to flush all of the toilets in the United States.

• • • •

A camel with a humongous thirst can gulp down as much as 28 gallons in ten minutes.

The Pentagon building has 685 water fountains.

• • • •

Word has it that there are only two words in the English language which end in "shion"- cushion and fashion.

• • • •

The covers of the first books of maps depicted Atlas holding the world on his back. That's why a book of maps is called an Atlas today.

• • • •

President Franklin Pierce was First Lady Barbara Bush's great-great-great-uncle. Her maiden name is Pierce.

• • • •

The average foil wrapper of a Hershey's Kiss measures five square inches.

• • • •

What common "bond" do celebrities Zsa Zsa Gabor, Stan Laurel, Mickey Rooney, Elizabeth Taylor and Lana Turner have? They've each been married eight times.

The life span of a one-dollar bill is about eighteen months.

• • • •

A kangaroo can hop more than 30 feet in a single bound.

• • • •

All even-numbered highways in the U.S. move east and west, while odd-numbered ones travel north and south.

• • • •

The U.S. Public Health Service says the three dog breeds which are least likely to bite are the golden retriever, Labrador, and the Shetland sheepdog.

• • • •

One armed bandits in China are called "hungry tigers".

Privia
The White House has 34 bathrooms.

Every summer, tens of millions of Americans are red-faced to find that they've come down with erythema. That's sunburn to non-medical types.

• • • •

Melt an ice cube in your mouth and you'll burn off 2.3 calories.

• • • •

Pablo Picasso's wife left him in 1963 when she learned he had recently been unfaithful. The artist was 82 years old at the time.

• • • •

Quick Quiz

Abraham Lincoln was shot dead, yet if it weren't for his son, the 16th President of the United States would never have been born. How can this be?

Ironically, President Lincoln's grandfather, also named Abraham, was killed by an Indian at his Kentucky farm. So, if it weren't for Abraham's son, Thomas Lincoln, the future president would never have existed.

• • • •

A slug travels about 50 yards a day.

Trivia Challenge #1

1. Whose picture was on the first U.S. postage stamp?

2. In what game is "OK" not OK?

3. True or false? Quitman, Texas, is the home of The Miss Ima Hogg Museum, named for the only daughter of Governor James T. Hogg.

4. Elizabeth Foster of fairy tale fame is commonly known by what other name?

5. On the spine of this book, you'll find a number preceded by the letters "ISBN". What do these initials stand for?

6. What was the world's tallest structure in the 19th century?

7. What state is Pittsburg in?

8. What shape is a stop sign? How about a yield sign? And a railroad crossing sign?

9. What is ethylene glycol commonly known as?

10. What is a "dead man's hand" in poker and, for extra credit, how did it get its name?

Answers

1. *Benjamin Franklin.*

2. *Scrabble.*

3. *Believe it or not, it's true. Visitors are "boared" with Hogg family paraphernalia and Texas memorabilia.*

4. *Mother Goose.*

5. *International Standard Book Number.*

6. *The Eiffel Tower.*

7. *Colorado, Kansas, Kentucky, New Hampshire, Oklahoma and Texas. There is, of course, a Pittsburgh, with an "h", in Pennsylvania.*

8. *Octagon, triangle, and circle.*

9. *Antifreeze.*

10. *Two pairs, aces and eights. Marshal Wild Bill Hickok was fatally shot in the back while holding this ill-fated hand.*

When a woodpecker pecks, its head travels at a speed of 1,300 miles per hour .

• • • •

H, I, N, O, S, X, and Z are the only letters of the alphabet which read the same upside down as rightside up.

• • • •

Kalamazoo, Michigan, is nicknamed the Celery City.

• • • •

On May 16, 1982, Jay Luo became the youngest college graduate ever when he received his B.S. from Idaho's Boise State. He was twelve.

Privia

Actress Joan Crawford changed her toilet seats every time she changed husbands.

• • • •

The most common name for a town in the United States is Fairview.

• • • •

Paul Revere was paid the equivalent of $23.59 for his midnight ride. We're not sure if that included overtime pay.

• • • •

You can draw a 35 mile line with the lead in an average pencil.

• • • •

Benjamin Franklin invented the school desk.

• • • •

Barbie's measurements are 5¼" - 3" - 4¾".

• • • •

Just before she was guillotined to death, Marie Antoinette stepped on her executioner's foot. Her last words were, "Pardon, sir. I did not do it on purpose."

Privia

Actor Lee Marvin was once
a plumber's apprentice.

The number one fear of most Americans is speaking
before a group.

• • • •

The only president to have been an Eagle Scout is
Gerald Ford.

• • • •

Only one out of six puppies finds a home.

• • • •

Americans peel about 12 billion bananas a year. That's
enough to make a banana split about 1.9 million miles
long!

• • • •

The shortest movie title ever belongs to a 1931 film directed by Fritz Lang: "M".

• • • •

Female bears give birth while they're asleep.

Privia

The following newspaper item comes from an edition of the *Philadelphia Inquirer:* "Donald Bollman was riding in a recreational vehicle with its owner when he asked to use the bathroom. His companion directed him to the rear, whereupon Bollman opened the moving vehicle's door and dropped out onto the Pennsylvania Turnpike."

• • • •

David Kunst went for a walk from June 10, 1970, to October 5, 1974 — around the world.

• • • •

George Washington died while taking his own pulse.

• • • •

The Name Game

Celebrities are famous for adopting stage names — Fred Austerlitz changed his last name to Astaire, Susan Kerr Weld changed her first name to Tuesday, and Wynette Pugh made her first name her surname and changed her first name to Tammy. While the previously mentioned names gave some hint of their alias, many of the famous created monickers entirely different than their original name. See if you can match those listed below.

1. Bo Diddley   a. Vincent Furnier

2. Charles Atlas   b. Aaron Chwatt

3. Lucille Ball   c. Sidney Liebowitz

4. Alice Cooper   d. Annie May Bullock

5. Boris Karloff   e. Sarah Ophelia Colley Cannon

6. Red Buttons   f. Angelo Siciliano

7. Lauren Bacall   g. Dianne Belmont

8. Minnie Pearl   h. Betty Joan Perske

9. Tina Turner   i. Elias McDaniel

10. Steve Lawrence   j. William Henry Pratt

Answers: 1, i; 2, f; 3, g; 4, a; 5, j; 6, b; 7, h; 8, e; 9, d; 10, c.

Americans spend more on cat food than baby food—about two billion dollars are spent annually.

• • • •

Athens, Carthage, Damascus, Egypt, England, Formosa, Genoa, Hamburg, Havana, Jerusalem, London, Manila, Moscow, Oxford, Palestine, Paris, Scotland, and Ulm are all places which can be found in the state of Arkansas.

• • • •

The cucumber has the fewest calories of all raw vegetables.

• • • •

There are over 9,000 television and radio stations in the U.S.

Privia

Actress Jodie Foster put her Oscar (for best actress) in her bathroom next to the tub.

What do Marlene Dietrich, Mike Nichols, Elke Sommer and Katherine Cornell have in common? They were all born in Berlin — no doubt because they wanted to be near their mothers.

There are forty spaces on a Monopoly game board.

•   •   •   •

U.S. President Grover Cleveland, when he was sheriff of Erie County, New York, twice served as a hangman.

•   •   •   •

You only get goosebumps on parts of your body that have hair.

•   •   •   •

Quick Quiz

What is the second shortest month of the year?

April. Because of daylight savings time, the clocks are pushed one hour ahead in April, making the month 29 days and 23 hours long.

•   •   •   •

Donald Duck has a sister named Dumbella.

•   •   •   •

CARE is an acronym for Cooperative for American Relief Everywhere.

Marconi was 21 when he invented the radio.

• • • •

First Lady Bess Truman was the first to have air conditioning installed in the White House.

• • • •

The winner of the second Boston Marathon, in 1898, was Ronald McDonald.

• • • •

Federal regulations prohibit a kite within 500 feet of a cloud.

Privia

36% of Americans listen to the radio in the bathroom.

• • • •

Muhammad Ali and Joe Frazier have not only shared the same ring on occasion, they share the same birthday — January 17th.

Literally translated, the Italian word "linguine" means "little tongues".

• • • •

Place whatever emphasis you like on this — The only city in the United States which spells itself with an exclamation point is Hamilton! in southern Ohio.

• • • •

According to *Money* magazine, men carry an average of $27 on them.

• • • •

William Shakespeare willed his "second best bed" to his wife.

• • • •

Mexico City is built on top of an underground reservoir and is sinking 6 to 8 inches every year.

• • • •

The brain is about two percent of your body weight.

Privial Pursuit #1

Test your bathroom knowledge with the plumber's dozen we've provided, then check your answers and weigh your smarts on the bathroom scale following the quiz.

1. The *Wall Street Journal* says that what percentage of Americans shave with disposable razors?
   a. 33%
   b. 50%
   c. 67%
   d. 80%

2. What city offers the world's only guided tour of its sewer system?

3. Bill Neal is credited with being the first to sail across the English Channel in what kind of vessel?

4. Who invented the electric dry shaver in 1931?
   a. King Camp Gillette
   b. Colonel Jacob Schick
   c. Lee Remington
   d. Earnie Shavers

5. Do you recall the name of J.P. "Big Bopper" Richardson's 1960 hit song that was inspired by a Dove soap commercial?

6. Do more people prefer to shower or to bathe?

7. True or false? The White House had a telephone before it had indoor plumbing.

8. Which was invented first, the pop-up tissue box or the toothbrush with synthetic bristles?

9. How many times daily does the average American visit the bathroom?

10. True or false? The abbreviation "B.O." for body odor was created as an advertising scheme to help peddle Lifebuoy Soap.

11. What sitcom character said, "There's (sic) three things I hate: the opera, the police station and cold toilet seats."

12. Toilet paper was invented in 1857 by:
    a. Joseph Gayetty
    b. Mr. Whipple
    c. Arthur Scott
    d. Dred Scott

13. In an average lifetime, who will step on the bathroom scale the most times, a man or a woman?

Answers

1. C.

2. Paris.

3. A bathtub. *(We understand that the voyage really drained him!)*

4. B.

5. "Running Bear" *(No, not "Running B-a-r-e")*.

6. You hit the nail on the proverbial shower head if you said "shower." A study of bathroom habits found that 86% of men prefer showering while with women it's a 70-30 proposition.

7. True.

8. The pop-up tissue box was invented by Andrew Olsen in 1921 while Dr. West's Miracle Tuft Toothbrush, in 1938, became the first toothbrush with synthetic bristles.

9. 6.

10. True.

11. Archie Bunker.

12. A.

13. The average man will weigh himself 9,815 times in a lifetime while a woman does so 8,491 times.

The Bathroom Scale

SCORE	RATING
0-2	Down the drain
3-5	Throw in the towel
6-8	Close shave
9-11	Razor-sharp
12-13	Royal Flush!

Privia

Researchers at the Gillette Safety Razor Company concluded that the average man in an average lifetime spends 3,350 hours shaving. If he didn't shave at all, his beard would be 30 feet long.

In 1921, White Castle became the first fast-food hamburger chain.

• • • •

The top-selling candy bar in the U.S. is Snickers.

• • • •

Your eyesight is sharpest at noontime.

• • • •

The only one of the five boroughs of New York City that is on the mainland of the United States is the Bronx.

• • • •

Brides do not walk down the aisle of a church. The center walkway is the nave. The aisles are on the sides.

• • • •

40% of dogs are overweight.

• • • •

Tycoon J. Paul Getty was once a sparring partner for Jack Dempsey.

• • • •

On this very day, if it's an average one in the United States, forty people will get hurt on trampolines around the country.

• • • •

The *Guinness Book of Records* has its own record. It is the book which is most often stolen from British Public Libraries.

• • • •

Yes, Eskimos do sometimes use refrigerators to keep food from freezing.

• • • •

Men are about five times more likely to stutter than women.

• • • •

President Calvin Coolidge installed an electric horse in his White House bedroom and rode it regularly.

Privia

38% of Americans sing in the shower (or bath).

• • • •

Bats have knees that bend backwards.

• • • •

Some avid kite flyers actually ply their sport underwater in scuba gear. At least then the kites won't get caught in trees! Wonder if their friends tell them to "Go dry a kite!"

• • • •

Attempted suicide used to be a capital crime in England. Those convicted would usually get the death sentence. Talk about deterrence!

• • • •

In 1975, a Florida man established a world's record by slurping up 588 oysters in just 17½ minutes.

• • • •

Can you match the animal with its group name?

1. bears	a. sounder
2. swine	b. ostentation or muster
3. cats	c. sloth or sleuth
4. kangaroos	d. clutter or chowder
5. peacocks	e. troop

(Answers: 1. c; 2. a; 3. d; 4. e; 5. b)

• • • •

Corned beef has no corn. It gets its name from the salt corns, or pellets, which originally preserved this kind of beef.

Privia

An upscale bath shop in London goes by the name of "Plush Flush".

If the Big Apple had the same amount of people per square mile as Alaska, the population of Manhattan would be 14.

• • • •

The average American laughs 410,078 times in a lifetime.

• • • •

One out of nine weddings occur in June.

• • • •

Virginia extends farther west than West Virginia — by 57 miles.

• • • •

"Alamo" is the Spanish word for the cottonwood tree. Many of them grew right there on the battlegrounds.

• • • •

Every day is "Fodder's Day" for African elephants which chaw on 300 to 400 pounds of fodder every 24 hours.

• • • •

Cats and dogs have similar life spans with a 15 year average. The rule of thumb most people use to measure a cat's or dog's age to the human equivalent is to multiply the pet's age by seven; however, a more accurate scale, developed by a veterinarian, follows:

Pet's Actual Age	Analogous Age to Humans
3 months	5 years
6 months	10 years
12 months	15 years
2 years	24 years
4 years	32 years
6 years	40 years
8 years	48 years
10 years	56 years
14 years	72 years
18 years	91 years
21 years	106 years

• • • •

A whale's heart beats only nine times a minute.

• • • •

The United Nations was originally called "Associated Powers". Winston Churchill thought of the new name.

• • • •

There are so many restaurants, eateries and food vendors in New York City it's been estimated that a New Yorker can dine out every night up until the age of 65 without patronizing the same establishment twice. All of which is great because by the time you start going around again, they'll probably have forgotten what a lousy tipper you were!

Two sisters in the United States in 1829, Susan and Deborah Tripp, tipped the bathroom scales at 205 and 124 pounds, respectively. Susan was five years old and her sister was three at the time.

• • • •

The stinky stuff a skunk squirts is ethanethiol.

• • • •

Count 'em — There are 26 states named on the back of a five-dollar bill. (You'll need a magnifying glass for this one!)

• • • •

The metal thing which a shoe salesperson uses to measure your feet is called the Brannock device.

• • • •

The average refrigerator has a life span of 17 years.

• • • •

17% of the ties sold each year are bought as Father's Day gifts.

Quick Quiz

In 1952 he was offered the presidency of Israel but turned it down saying, "I know a little about nature and hardly anything about men." Who was this?

Albert Einstein.

• • • •

In almost all of the world's languages, the word for "mother" begins with the letter "m".

• • • •

The only major sport that is original to the U.S. is basketball.

• • • •

Some things are hard to keep a lid on: Every 2.7 seconds a new Tupperware party gets under way somewhere in the world.

• • • •

Abraham Lincoln moved his lips while reading.

• • • •

You grow close to ³/₁₀ of an inch at night but shrink back to your daytime height after you wake up.

• • • •

Queen Elizabeth II is the richest woman in the world with an estimated worth of nine billion dollars.

Privia

Ever wonder why hotels fold over the last piece of toilet paper in the bathroom? It's so the guest, in a very subtle way, is aware that the maid has cleaned the room and no one has used the bathroom since then.

• • • •

The average American will eat 1,889 Tootsie Rolls in his or her life.

• • • •

Richard Nixon is a descendant of England's King Edward III.

• • • •

Trivia Challenge #2

1. What's the highest denomination of U.S. currency ever printed? Whose face is on the bill?

2. What is a funambulist?

3. Name the world's largest residence occupied by one person.

4. Why were most of the little school houses of yesteryear painted red?

5. True or false? A U.S. President and Vice-President cannot be from the same state.

6. Melvin Cowznofski was the original name of what demented magazine's unflappable cover boy?

7. When does the number 14 fall between 9 and 11?

8. For years, Maxwell House coffee has been telling us that it's "Good to the last drop." Who came up with this famous slogan?
   a. Stan Freberg
   b. Noel Coward
   c. Dorothy Parker
   d. Theodore Roosevelt

9. What's wrong with "Pike's Peak" as it appears in this sentence?

10. This state's three largest cities start with the letter "C." Name it.

Answers

1. $100,000. Woodrow Wilson's face graces it. (This bill was never circulated. It was used solely for transactions between the Treasury Department and the Federal Reserve.)

2. A tightrope walker.

3. The Vatican.

4. Elementary . . . red was the cheapest color of paint.

5. True.

6. "Mad" magazine's Alfred E. Neuman. ("What, me worry?")

7. When it's on a dart board.

8. D. Good thing he didn't say, "Bully to the last drop!"

9. Colorado lawmakers mandated that the apostrophe be banished. Period.

10. Ohio. (Columbus, Cleveland, and Cincinnati - in that order.)

Every week, the President of the United States receives 140,000 letters.

• • • •

It's nothing to be embarrassed about, but when your face blushes so does your stomach lining.

Privia

In his/her lifetime, the average American will use up to 410,078 gallons of water in the bathroom sink, 546,770 gallons for showers and/or baths, and a whopping 1,093,540 gallons of water in flushing the toilet.

• • • •

When George Eastman, the inventor of the Kodak camera, committed suicide in 1932 he left this note: "To My Friends: My work is done. Why wait?"

• • • •

There is only one whole number than can be added to itself or multiplied by itself and still get the same result — and that number is 2. (2x2=4 or 2+2=4)

• • • •

The population of the United States in 1801 was around five million people. 20 percent of them were slaves.

• • • •

Butterflies are cannibals.

• • • •

Procrastinating Pigeon: William S. Wellman of Cleveland, Ohio, entered his new homing pigeon in a hundred mile race in 1939. The bird didn't do so well. In fact, it finished last. In fact, it didn't return home until 1948.

• • • •

Silent Cal Coolidge always lived up to his reputation. A woman sat next to him at a dinner gathering and said, "You must talk to me, Mr. Coolidge. I made a bet today that I could get more than two words out of you." The former U.S. President replied: "You lose."

• • • •

The world's record for keeping a Lifesaver in the mouth with the hole intact is 7 hours and 10 minutes.

• • • •

Elvis Presley made just one TV commercial — in 1954, for Southern Doughnuts.

• • • •

The Statue of Liberty wears sandals.

• • • •

He's Sao Nicolau in Brazil, Papa Koleda in Bulgaria, Befana in Italy, Julenissen in Denmark — and in the good ol' U.S. of A., he's known as Santa Claus.

• • • •

The only vegetable or fruit which is never sold in any other form than fresh is lettuce.

• • • •

Most spiders have eight eyes arranged on the head to enable them to see in all directions at once.

• • • •

By the time George Washington became president, he had only one tooth left—a lower-right bicuspid.

• • • •

When daredevil Evel Knievel did his very first stunt jump into the world, his mother named him Robert Craig Knievel.

• • • •

Patriot Patrick Henry left his entire estate to his wife with one major stipulation- that she never remarry. Mrs. Henry remarried, fought the will in court and won.

Privia

Statistics show that on an average day in America no less than 90 people will require emergency room treatment for a toilet and/or sink accident.

• • • •

No only child has become President of the United States.

• • • •

The plural of mongoose is mongooses.

• • • •

The total number of gifts in the song *The Twelve Days of Christmas* is 364.

You probably already knew this, you just never thought about it. Batteries *do* wear out faster if you turn up the volume on a radio.

• • • •

A giraffe has the same number of bones in its neck as a human.

• • • •

What do Tony Bennett, Jack Klugman, Burt Lancaster, Peter Finch and Rudolph Valentino have in common? They all worked as waiters before fate served up success.

• • • •

John Quincy Adams owned a pet alligator which he kept in the East Room of the White House.

• • • •

The comic strip *Peanuts* is known as *Little Radishes* in Denmark.

• • • •

Martin Luther King, Jr.'s mother was also murdered. She was shot to death while playing the organ in church in 1974, six years after her son was assassinated.

The most prevalent crime committed by women is shoplifting.

• • • •

A color TV's life expectancy is 8 years.

• • • •

The medical term for yawning is pandiculating.

• • • •

According to Hostess sources, Twinkie inventor Jimmy Dewar ate 40,177 Twinkies during his life.

Privia

A newspaper in St. John, New Brunswick, Canada, once reported that a man was sentenced to 30 days in jail for stealing three boxes of Ex-Lax. His name: Frederick Andrew Outhouse.

• • • •

The state of Maine is the world's largest producer of toothpicks.

Privial Pursuit #2

Time to take #2 — another set of bathroom bafflers. To see how flush you are with success, refer to The Bathroom Scale which followed Privial Pursuit #1.

1. A shaving cream manufacturer had some 600 jingles which lined highway billboards from the Thirties through the Fifties. One such roadside campaign was:
        I know
        He's a wolf
        Said Riding Hood
        But Grandma dear,
        He smells so Good
        (Fill in the name here.)

2. In 1517, Francis I of France purchased this to hang in his bathroom.

3. According to the title of Erma Bombeck's best-selling book in the late 70's, where is the grass always greener?

4. What is the most popular toothbrush color?

5. "It-kills-germs-by-the-millions-on-contact" is the slogan of what mouthwash?

6. What comedienne once said, "I knew I was unwanted when I saw that my bath toys were a toaster and a radio"?

7. During World War II, a common French saying was "Je vais telephoner a Hitler". What was the American equivalent of that?

8. The wife of what famous composer orchestrated the development of the johnny mop?

9. Where was President John F. Kennedy when he put the finishing touches on his Inaugural Address?

10. What singing artist made the 1970 recording of *She Came In Through The Bathroom Window*?

11. What is the average life span of a bathroom scale?
    a.   5 years
    b.   10 years
    c.   15 years
    d.   20 years

12. "If you don't mind smelling like a peanut for two or three days, peanut butter is a darn good shaving cream." This quote is attributed to an ex-presidential candidate. Who is he?

13. What TV commercial made actress Jane Withers a star?

Answers

1. *Burma-Shave.*

2. *The Mona Lisa.*

3. *"The Grass Is Always Greener Over The Septic Tank".*

4. *Blue.*

5. *Listerine.*

6. *Joan Rivers.*

7. *"I'm going to see a man about a horse (or a dog)."*

8. *Richard Rodgers.*

9. *In the bathtub.*

10. *Joe Cocker.*

11. *B.*

12. *Barry Goldwater.*

13. *Maybe we should have said "made her a comet". Comet cleanser was the product that she endorsed as Josephine the Plumber.*

Quick Quiz

Who was the first President of the United States to have a child born in the White House?

Grover Cleveland. His daughter Ruth even had a candy bar named after her — the Baby Ruth.

• • • •

Dwight D. Eisenhower would customarily wear three coats of clear nail polish.

• • • •

The word "video" is Latin for "I see".

• • • •

The most frequently used letters in the English language are e, t, o, a, and n in that order.

• • • •

The country where you have the fattest chance of being overweight is the United States.

• • • •

Giraffes give birth standing up.

Quick Quiz

Can you name four United States Presidents who wore beards when elected?

Ulysses S. Grant, Rutherford B. Hayes, James A. Garfield and Benjamin Harrison. Lincoln grew a beard after he was already in office.

• • • •

If you look at the back of a $10 bill, you'll see a car in front of the U.S. Treasury building. It's a 1926 Hupmobile.

• • • •

Rin Tin Tin is buried under a black onyx tombstone which says "The Greatest Cinema Star". The canine celebrity was laid to rest in a Paris, France, cemetery.

• • • •

An airplane's black box is orange.

• • • •

"The whole nine yards" comes from a masonry term which referred to the nine cubic yards of cement which was the capacity of some cement-mixer trucks.

Jim Thorpe's Indian name was Bright Path.

• • • •

About one out of seven Americans has no health insurance.

Privia

Salmon P. Chase, Abraham Lincoln's Secretary of the Treasury, was a religious sort who was known for quoting psalms in the bathtub. He was also responsible for the motto "In God We Trust" on U.S. coins.

• • • •

Gargling is not permitted on television according to the National Association of Broadcasters.

• • • •

Zip a dee doo dah: Newton Falls, Ohio, lays claim to the only single-repeating-digit zip code: 44444.

• • • •

During World War II, Pope John XXIII was a sergeant in the Italian Army.

Lavatory Laws

From City Hall to bathroom stall, here's a hodgepodge of silly statutes which were — and in some cases, may still be — in existence around the U.S.

A Bexley, Ohio, law prohibits slot machines in outhouses.

• • • •

An old Virginia ordinance forbids putting bathtubs in the house. They could only be kept in the yard.

• • • •

You're breaking the law if you fall asleep in a bathtub in Detroit, Michigan.

• • • •

Until December, 1978, a Connecticut regulation required all toilets to have horseshoe-shaped seats.

• • • •

In Poplar Bluff, Missouri, a man with a five o'clock shadow must wait until six. Shaving in the daytime is against the law.

A Brooklyn, New York, statute forbids donkeys to doze in the bathtub.

• • • •

Residents of Barre, Vermont, were once required by a town ordinance to bathe every night. And Kentucky citizens, whether they wanted to or not, were obligated by law to take a bath at least once a year.

• • • •

Unless you have permission from him, sleeping in a neighbor's outhouse in San Jose, California, is against the law. And smoking a cigar in a St. John's, Newfoundland, outhouse is a definite no-no.

• • • •

A Carmel, California, law prohibits a woman from taking a bath in a business office.

• • • •

It's illegal to wear roller skates in a Portland, Oregon, restroom.

• • • •

Suffolk County, Long Island, prohibits mobile hot-dog stands unless there's a bathroom in the immediate vicinity.

• • • •

Stealing soap is a dirty crime in Mojave, Arizona. Thieves caught pilfering soap must come clean by washing with it until it's all used up.

• • • •

In Minneapolis, Minnesota, you're not allowed to install a bathtub unless it has legs.

• • • •

Privia

Actor/comedian Chevy Chase, born Cornelius Crane Chase, is heir to the Crane Urinal fortune so, as far as cash goes, you could say he is "flush".

Volvo, as in the car, is Latin for "I roll".

• • • •

There are 1.4 million Avon sales representatives.

• • • •

Quick now — How many states are named after a president? Just one: Washington.

• • • •

It cost the Wright Brothers less than one thousand dollars to build their first airplane.

• • • •

Greenland is only ten miles from Canada.

Quick Quiz

"I used never to be able to get along. I used to feel that the teachers did not sympathize with me and that my father thought I was stupid." In his own words, that was why he only had three months of formal schooling before running away at the age of seven in 1854. Rather than shed any further light on our subject, can you guess who he is?

Thomas Edison.

The only word in the English language which can be formed by rearranging the letters in the word "pictures" is "piecrust".

•   •   •   •

Elvis Presley and his mother both died at the age of 42.

•   •   •   •

The only coin on which a president's head faces to the left is the Lincoln penny.

•   •   •   •

To Zane Grey, writing books was like pulling teeth — but he liked it better than pulling teeth so he gave up his career in dentistry and traded in his pliers for a typewriter.

•   •   •   •

Aside from being First Ladies, Martha Washington, Abigail Fillmore, Caroline Harrison, Florence Harding and Pat Nixon had at least one other thing in common. They were all older than their husbands.

•   •   •   •

Trivia Challenge #3

1. Here's a beauty of a question from the 60's. What do the following women have in common: Lynda Lee Mead, Nancy Fleming, Maria Fletcher, Jacquelyn Mayer, Donna Axum, Vonda Kay Van Dyke, Deborah Irene Bryant, Jane Anne Jayroe, Debra Denc Barnes, and Judith Anne Ford?

2. Who were Gaspar, Melchior, and Balthasar?

3. True or false? Three major television networks — ABC, NBC, and CBS — once covered a murder — live.

4. What bears the inscription, "Here rests in honored glory an American soldier known but to God"?

5. What are the dots on dice called?

6. Why couldn't Lassie have any puppies?

7. Food for thought: Alfred Packer is the only man in the U.S. to have been convicted of what crime?

8. Here's a stage name stumper: Who are Robert and Ethel Zimmerman?

9. Which one of the seven dwarfs was beardless?

10. Who is buried in Grant's tomb?

Answers

1. *They all strolled down the runway as Miss America — from 1960-69, respectively.*

2. *The Three Wise Men.*

3. *True. It was Jack Ruby's shooting of Lee Harvey Oswald.*

4. *The Tomb of the Unknown Soldier.*

5. *Pips.*

6. *All the dogs who played the canine TV star were males.*

7. *Cannibalism.*

8. *Bob Dylan and Ethel Merman. (We never said they were related.)*

9. *Dopey.*

10. *You're only half right if you answered Ulysses. The Mrs., Julia B., is also entombed there.*

Dwarf, dwell, and dwindle are the only words in the English language which begin with "dw".

• • • •

In the U.S., a trillion has 12 zeroes but that's a mere billion in Britain. The Brits' trillion — and the Germans' too — is equal to our quintillion. Something to keep in mind if you borrow money overseas!

• • • •

The hair on your head grows about 8 inches a year.

• • • •

The fastest bullet travels only about $\frac{1}{7}$ of the earth's escape velocity and nowhere near as fast as most spacecraft.

• • • •

For many years there was an "ugliness" ordinance in Chicago which forbade anyone who was disfigured, deformed or unsightly to be seen or displayed in public.

• • • •

If Mom is colorblind and Dad has normal vision, their daughters will have normal vision but their sons will be colorblind.

• • • •

The maiden name of comic-strip star Blondie Bumstead is Boopadoop.

• • • •

Quick Quiz

You might say that Annie Ide was Robert Louis Stevenson's calendar girl. What rather unique bequest did Stevenson make to his lady friend?

As she was always complaining about having been born on Christmas Day, he left her his birthday, November 13.

• • • •

Rather odd is the town in Missouri called Peculiar.

• • • •

A million dollars in 100 dollar bills weighs about 20 pounds.

• • • •

The hyoid bone, which is in the throat and supports the tongue and its muscles, is the only bone that does not connect with any other in the body.

• • • •

Elephants have a trunk so flexible that some of them can even untie a knot with it.

• • • •

It's estimated that by the time a child reaches the age of eighteen, he/she will have watched more than 17,000 hours of TV.

• • • •

Australian lifeguards wear pantyhose to protect themselves against jellyfish.

Privia

The ingredients are water, chalk, titanium dioxide, glycerin glycol, seaweed and paraffin oil, detergent, peppermint oil and saccharin, and formaldehyde. The result: toothpaste.

Ruth Rasmussen of Traer, Iowa, is the salt of the earth. In fact, you might say that she's a woman for all seasonings as she has amassed a collection of well over 12,000 sets of salt and pepper shakers since 1946.

• • • •

Cholesterol makes up one seventh of the human brain and spinal cord.

• • • •

George Washington refused to shake hands, preferring to bow instead.

• • • •

In the mid 1970's at Florida's Derby Lane greyhound track, one of the top dogs was Cilohocla. The origin of the dog's name was a mystery until someone reversed its spelling.

• • • •

Ants can pull up to 52 times their own weight.

• • • •

Bottled beer is colder than canned beer.

• • • •

It takes about 548 peanuts to make a 12 ounce jar of peanut butter.

Quick Quiz

The only people in the Baseball Hall of Fame who have nothing to do with the game are Abbott and Costello for their "Who's on First?" comedy routine. Can you name their starting lineup?

First base, Who; second base, What; third base, I Don't Know; shortstop, I Don't Give a Darn (or I Don't Care); catcher, Today; pitcher, Tomorrow; left field, Why; center field, Because. There was no right fielder in the routine.

• • • •

The reason "lb." is an abbreviation for 16 ounces is that it is a contraction of "libra", the Latin word for pound.

• • • •

Americans drink more wine on Thanksgiving than any other day.

The Teacup Chihuahua is the smallest dog in the world. It weighs less than a pound and can stand in the palm of your hand.

• • • •

The northernmost of the 48 contiguous United States is Minnesota.

• • • •

The average American opens the refrigerator door 22 times a day.

• • • •

Camp David, the presidential retreat, was called Shangri-La until President Eisenhower renamed it after his grandson in 1953.

• • • •

Privia

Only one in six families had a bathtub in the 1880s. In fact, the majority of Americans didn't have a bathtub until after World War I.

Thomas Jefferson died bankrupt.

• • • •

For some unknown reason, mosquitoes are attracted to the color blue far more than any other.

• • • •

It was the biggest island in the world and also just about the coldest, so to make it sound more attractive to potential settlers, naming it was black and white to discoverer Eric the Red — Greenland.

• • • •

From 1949 to 1951, the Temple University Owls had a basketball player who was known as "the Owl without a vowel" — William Mlkvy.

• • • •

The average garden variety caterpillar has 228 muscles in its head.

• • • •

Idaho isn't way up there on the list of tourism states probably because of that long-standing law they had banning fishing for trout from the back of a giraffe!

Sports - 20 Questions

1. In golf, what is a double albatross?

2. How far apart are neighboring bowling pins?

3. Who was the model for the Heisman Trophy?

4. What is the life span of a baseball during a major league game?

5. We think we can pin you to the mat on this one. Who is Terry Jean Bollette?

6. On what two days of the year are there never any major professional or college games being played?

7. What was the reason the Yankees first wore pinstripes?

8. How thick is a hockey puck?

9. Where do the lakes in the NBA's Los Angeles Lakers come from?

10. What is the origin of the term "doubleheader"?

11. What is the official name for the bird in badminton?

12. Name the player who was the model for the NBA's silhouette logo.

13. The doorbell of former pitcher Tommy John plays what tune?

14. According to recent studies, what magazine is most likely to be stolen from public libraries in the U.S.?

15. How many people were in the stands in Mudville that day when Mighty Casey went down on strikes?

16. The *International Lawn Tennis Challenge Trophy* is better known by what name?

17. Wally Pipp and Babe Dahlgren were like bookends to what epic story?

18. Would Carl Lewis record a faster time running the 220 yard dash or running one furlong?

19. Cleveland Indian Hall-of-Famer Bob Feller threw a no-hitter against Chicago yet none of the White Sox' batting averages changed. How can that be?

20. Let's play *Jeopardy* . . . In 1942, less than a month after the Japanese attacked Pearl Harbor, it was decided to move the game to a less vulnerable site. The contest between Oregon State and Duke was hosted by Duke in Durham, North Carolina. Oregon State won, 20-16. And the question is . . .

Sports – 20 Questions (Answers)

1. *Two successive holes in one.*

2. *12 inches.*

3. *It's first winner, Jay Berwanger.*

4. *Seven pitches.*

5. *Terry Jean Bollette is the real name of wrestling's Hulk Hogan.*

6. *The day before and the day after the Major League Baseball All-Star Game.*

7. *Because of Babe Ruth's weight. Owner Jacob Ruppert, in 1925, decided to order pinstripes for the team's uniforms to make the 260 pound Bambino look thinner — thus was born a tradition.*

8. *One inch (no matter what Don Rickles says).*

9. *From Minnesota, when they used to play in Minneapolis.*

10. *It derives from railroad jargon. Doubleheader is lingo for a train with two engines.*

11. *A shuttlecock.*

12. *Jerry West.*

13. *"Take Me Out to the Ball Game".*

14. *"Sports Illustrated".*

15. *5,000 ("10,000 eyes were on him.")*

16. *The Davis Cup.*

17. *Lou Gehrig's 2,130 consecutive games played. They were the "before and after" first basemen.*

18. *They are the same distance.*

19. *It was opening day (the only opening day no-hitter ever thrown).*

20. *What is the Rose Bowl?*

Three females have appeared on U.S. currency: Martha Washington, on the 1886 and 1891 $1 certificates and on the 1896 silver certificate; Pocahontas, on the back of the 1875 $20 bill; and Susan B. Anthony, on the 1979 silver dollar.

Quick Quiz

What is the significance of Cape Three Points? Hint: If you're next to nowhere with an answer, you're right.

Located on the Gulf of Guinea near West Africa, Cape Three Points is called "The Land Nearest Nowhere". It is the closest land area to a spot in the sea where zero longitude and zero latitude converge at zero altitude.

•   •   •   •

Do you know the faces of Gutzon Borglum? Sure you do — he's the artist who carved Mount Rushmore.

•   •   •   •

Deviled eggs are so-called because when they were first made they were covered with such hot pepper that it supposedly reminded one of the fires of hell.

•   •   •   •

In a box of Cracker Jacks, there are nine nuts per ounce.

Donald Duck's middle name is Fauntleroy.

• • • •

Cross a grapefruit with a tangerine and you get an ugli fruit. No, that's not a value judgment. That's the name of the hybrid fruit grown primarily in Jamaica. It's a much sweeter and bumpier version of the grapefruit.

• • • •

The French call cotton candy "Papa's Beard".

• • • •

The average American, in a lifetime, spends six months waiting for red lights to change.

• • • •

Harry S Truman had a bowling alley installed in the basement of the White House.

• • • •

Erich Weiss, a.k.a. the famed magician Harry Houdini, made his final disappearing act on Halloween.

Privia

In exile on St. Helena, Napoleon would take as many as three baths a day, some lasting several hours.

• • • •

Franklin D. Roosevelt was a notorious practical joker. At White House functions, he realized that no one really paid attention to the brief pleasantries exchanged so on one occasion, as he shook hands with each guest he muttered, "I murdered my grandmother this morning." Only one guest, a Wall Street banker, responded. He said, "She certainly had it coming!"

• • • •

The largest variety of pumpkin in the world is Dill's Atlantic Giant which commonly grows to 800 pounds or more.

• • • •

Hedy Lamarr held a patent for a torpedo guidance system, Paul Winchell invented an artificial heart and bandleader Fred Waring gave the world the Waring Blender.

• • • •

Presidential trivia: What does the number 66 have to do with the first five presidents? That's the age at which Washington, Adams, Jefferson, Madison and Monroe left office.

Privia

If your bathroom faucet drips at the rate of just one drop per second, you'll be wasting 900 gallons of water in a year.

• • • •

A tongue-twisting fact: Turtles are toothless.

• • • •

"To put it mildly, this was an oddball." — You have just read the entire biography of George Armstrong Custer, as written by James Warner Bellah.

• • • •

During the 1949 to 1957 run of *The Lone Ranger* on television, Clayton Moore was not the only Kemosabe in town. John Hart also played the Masked Man for a couple of seasons.

• • • •

The average person sleeps about 2,920 hours each year. Figured on a 70 year life span, that's 204,400 hours or about 23 years.

• • • •

It takes 40,000 pounds of potatoes to make 14,000 pounds of chips.

• • • •

Alfred C. Gilbert, the inventor of the Erector Set, was also a doctor, an Olympic gold medalist in the pole vault and a famed big game hunter.

Quick Quiz

What is the only country in the world that is populated but where no one is born?

Vatican City. The world's smallest independent state has a population of about 1,000.

• • • •

The 1950 Nash was the first automobile to sport seat belts.

• • • •

Off the Wall

Graffiti found on bathroom walls around the world

Hypochondria is the only disease I haven't got.

• • • •

The other line always moves faster.

• • • •

If doesn't matter whether you win or lose — until you lose.

• • • •

Joan of Arc was Noah's wife.

• • • •

Jesus saves, but Gretzky scores on the rebound.

• • • •

Celibacy is not hereditary.

Betsy Ross was a sew & sew.

• • • •

The future isn't what it used to be.

• • • •

Support wildlife — throw a party.

• • • •

Where there's a will there's a delay.

• • • •

I fixed Olivia Newton's john.

• • • •

If Ella Fitzgerald married Darth Vader, she'd be Ella . . .

• • • •

No job is complete 'til the paperwork is done.

Where you stand on an issue depends where you sit.

• • • •

A bird in hand is safer than one overhead.

• • • •

People who write on bathroom walls need psychological treatment.

• • • •

Obesity is widespread.

• • • •

Unemployment isn't working.

• • • •

Schizophrenia beats dining alone.

• • • •

Plumbers have pipe dreams.

Jack and Jill are over the hill.

• • • •

John Doe is a nobody.

• • • •

Join the Army, see the world, meet interesting people — and kill them.

• • • •

The reverse side also has a reverse side.

• • • •

Weightlifters are biceptual.

Mt. Everest is 29,000 feet high, to the inch. Worried that the public might think this was an estimated height, surveyors falsely reported that it was 29,002 feet.

• • • •

Christmas is abbreviated as Xmas because the Greek letter x is the first letter of the Greek word for Christ, Xristos. Xmas means "Christ's Mass" and was commonly used in Europe. The abbreviation was not, as many people think, meant to take Christ out of the celebration.

• • • •

In Toronto, there was a backlash against Mensa and some folks of modest IQs formed a club called "Densa" where the main activities were watching TV and going to sporting events.

• • • •

Harvey Kennedy patented the shoelace and walked all the way to the bank with $2.5 million from it.

• • • •

Kleenex researchers say the average person blows his/her nose 256 times a year.

What's in a name? Hot off the Associated Press wires in 1976 was the news that Richard Nixon was arrested in Pittsburgh for suspicion of marijuana. George Washington was the arresting officer. Washington's partner, Benjamin Franklin, would also have been there if he hadn't been sick.

• • • •

Next time you hear the term "civilized world" remember that historians have calculated that in the last 3500 years, there have been only 230 years of peace.

• • • •

When J.C. Penney (middle name Cash) opened his first department store in 1902, it was called The Golden Rule.

• • • •

The most popular name for a pope is John. There have been 23 Pope Johns (25 if you count the 2 John Pauls).

• • • •

The most dangerous ride in the amusement park? Forget the cyclone, the loop-de-loop, or any of the frightful roller coaster rides. The most hazardous ride of them all is . . . the merry go round which accounts for more accidents than any other single ride!

"Lenin" was an alias. The leader of the Russian Revolution's real name was Ulyanov.

• • • •

A rose is a rose or is it? The Harlem Globetrotters started out in Chicago . . . Cashew nuts are not nuts; they're a fruit . . . The French poodle came from Germany.

Privia

License plates in Hot Springs, Arkansas, once featured a bathtub and the slogan "We Bathe the World".

• • • •

Da Vinci, Michelangelo and Picasso were all southpaws.

• • • •

Kenny Baker, whose career has literally been "in the can" as R2D2 in the *Star Wars* trilogy, is all of 2 feet, 8 inches tall.

• • • •

Venice, Italy, has 400 bridges.

• • • •

Double check that restaurant bill. There's a 1 in 8 chance that it's incorrect.

• • • •

A couple of heavy hitters shared the same plane in bombing missions over Korea. Co-piloting with former astronaut John Glenn, was baseball Hall of Famer Ted Williams.

• • • •

The average worker in the U.S. in 1905 made $523.12 a year.

• • • •

If you're ever in Cedar City, Utah, and you're over 50, don't get caught drinking beer with your shoelaces untied or you'll run afoul of the law.

• • • •

More phone calls are placed on Mother's Day than on any other day in the year in the U.S.

December 7th is remembered as "Pearl Harbor Day", a date which will live in infamy. On the other hand, December 7th marks the beginning of the U.S.A. as Delaware became the first state by ratifying the Constitution on that day in 1787.

• • • •

VANITY PL8S

Can you identify the people who own the following license plates?

1. Y R U FATT

2. X CZECH

3. XXOF

4. WDSTK-1

5. H2O GATE

6. AGT MAX

1. Richard Simmons 2. Martina Navratilova (now a U.S. citizen) 3. Redd Foxx (last name spelled backwards) 4. Charles Schulz (as in Woodstock) 5. G. Gordon Liddy (for Watergate) 6. Don Adams (for his Maxwell Smart TV role).

• • • •

A mnemonic for remembering the planets in order of their distance from the sun is "My Very Earnest Mother Just Served Us Nine Pickles" — Mercury, Venus, Earth, Mars, Jupiter, Saturn, Uranus, Neptune, and Pluto.

Trivia Challenge #4

1. What did John Quincy Adams, Rutherford B. Hayes and Benjamin Harrison each win and lose at the same time?

2. Which chef invented potato chips in 1853?
   a. Samuel French
   b. Bruce Fries
   c. George Crum
   d. Chip Hilton

3. True or false? The book *.007* was one of the James Bond series written by Ian Fleming.

4. From what nickel and dime operation did the giant K-Mart chain evolve?

5. The Chinese have some 50,000 of them — or 49,974 more than we do. What?

6. What is the plural of the word "moose"?

7. Two teenagers, Jerry Siegel and Joe Shuster, created what heroic figure of American literature?

8. Lake Havasu City, Arizona, is the second home of what famous landmark?

9. How many eyes are on a dollar bill?

10. Baloney was first served in Bologna, Italy. Is this statement factual or is it baloney itself?

Answers

1. *They all won the Presidential election by way of the Electoral College but lost as far as the popular vote was concerned.*

2. *C.*

3. *False. Ian Fleming's book didn't have a decimal point. ".007" was a Rudyard Kipling story.*

4. *S.S. Kresge. (K=Kresge.)*

5. *Letters of the alphabet.*

6. *Moose.*

7. *They created a bird, a plane... no, they created Superman.*

8. *The London Bridge. It was disassembled in London, transported to the States, then rebuilt and reopened in 1971.*

9. *Four. (On the front are Washington's two eyes; on the back, one eye of the eagle is shown and there's the "Eye of Providence" over the pyramid.)*

10. *True.*

In 1873, Mark Twain was granted a patent for the self-pasting scrapbook.

•   •   •   •

The first names of Dr. Jekyll and Mr. Hyde in the Robert Louis Stevenson classic were Henry and Edward, respectively.

•   •   •   •

The average person will drink about 16,000 gallons of water in a lifetime.

Privia

The *Sunday Independent*, a Wilkes-Barre, Pennsylvania, newspaper, once reported a story about a woman who returned home after a hospital stay "and found the first-floor rear door to her home forced open. In a search of the home, the only article found missing was a four-pack of Charmin toilet tissue."

•   •   •   •

Who wrote *The Star Spangled Banner*? Francis Scott Key? Half-right. He wrote the words. The tune was written many years before by an Englishman named John Stafford Smith.

• • • •

Alaska is the only state in the U.S. where houseflies don't live.

• • • •

Long before he got into big-time trouble for tax evasion, former baseball great Pete Rose got a two-bit ticket for parking illegally on a street outside Cincinnati's Riverfront Stadium. The street name — Pete Rose Way.

• • • •

To Paul Revere, Betsy Ross and J. Edgar Hoover, January 1st rang in the New Year in more ways than one. It was also their birthday.

• • • •

The average American makes between three and four phone calls a day.

• • • •

Privia

Otto Schnering, creator of the Baby Ruth, leased a small room over a plumber's shop in Chicago just before World War I. This was his first headquarters for the Curtiss Candy Company.

• • • •

The Washington Monument is sinking into the ground at the rate of about a foot every other century.

• • • •

Some years ago a New Zealand man was convicted of murdering his wife by stabbing her with a frozen sausage. The court no doubt "meted" out severe punishment.

• • • •

By an 1893 Supreme Court decision, the tomato was declared a vegetable, not a fruit.

• • • •

The primary flavorings in Juicy Fruit gum are, in no particular order since the proportions are a trade secret: banana, lemon, pineapple and orange.

• • • •

The first U.S. President to drive a car was Warren G. Harding.

• • • •

Rembrandt's last name was van Rijn.

• • • •

325 pound William Howard Taft was the biggest president (so big he once got stuck in the White House bathtub). When he was governor-general of the Philippines, he sent the following cable to Secretary of War Elihu Root: "TOOK LONG HORSEBACK RIDE TODAY. FEELING FINE." Root responded in kind: "HOW IS THE HORSE?"

• • • •

Privia

England's King George II died after he fell off a toilet.

Privia

An all-important statistical survey found that 88% of Americans say they'd replace an empty roll of toilet tissue rather than leave the chore to the next person.

• • • •

Rocky Lane was the voice of Mr. Ed.

• • • •

A shrimp's heart rules its head — probably because that's exactly where it is!

• • • •

In a lifetime, Americans spend an average of 49 hours seeing doctors while spending 64 hours waiting to see them.

• • • •

7% of America eats at McDonald's every day.

• • • •

Winston Churchill was born in a ladies' cloakroom.

Bathroom Banter

The things people say about the places people go . . .

All my good reading, you might say, was done in the toilet. There are passages of "Ulysses" which can be read only in the toilet — if one wants to extract the full flavor of their content.

—Henry Miller

• • • •

A human being is an ingenious assembly of portable plumbing.

—Christopher Morley

• • • •

It's spring in England. I missed it last year. I was in the bathroom.

—Michael Flanders

• • • •

Hollywood is like Picasso's bathroom.

—Candice Bergen

• • • •

My family tree was chopped down and they made the lumber into toilet paper. We've never been closer.
—Barry Steiger

• • • •

According to statistics, a man eats a prune every twenty seconds. I don't know who this fella is, but I know where to find him.
—Morey Amsterdam

• • • •

Today you can go to a gas station and find the cash register open and the toilets locked. They must think toilet paper is worth more than money.
—Joey Bishop

• • • •

The Rose Bowl is the only bowl I've ever seen that I didn't have to clean.
—Erma Bombeck

• • • •

I'd like to be rich enough so I could throw soap away after the letters are worn off.

—Andy Rooney

• • • •

My bathroom has a digital sink. When I want to stop the water from running, I put my finger in the faucet.

—Ron Smith

• • • •

Running is an unnatural act, except from enemies and to the bathroom.

—Anonymous

• • • •

I just bought a new house. It has no plumbing. It's uncanny.

—Morey Amsterdam

• • • •

Most of the time he (Marlon Brando) sounds like he has a mouth full of wet toilet paper.

—Rex Reed

• • • •

I'm terribly lazy. That's why I love being in movies. I'm performing all over the world - while I'm home taking a bath.

—Barbra Streisand

• • • •

May your life be like a roll of toilet paper — long and useful.

—Anonymous

Quick Quiz

In 1664, the Dutch paid homage to Peter Stuyvesant with a full military burial even though he was very much alive. In 1842, Mexican leader Santa Anna was given the same tribute. For what were they given this ceremonial treatment? (Hint: You'll have to go out on a limb for this one.)

Their amputated legs.

The standard size of a credit card is 3⅜" by 2⅛".

• • • •

Here's something to chew on: 92% of Americans have bitten their fingernails at one time or another.

• • • •

That's a crocodile, not an alligator, which you see on an Izod Lacoste polo shirt. The physical difference between the two is in the snout—a crocodile's snout comes to a point while an alligator's is rounded.

• • • •

The tuxedo was introduced in 1886 by Griwold Lorillard at where else? — Tuxedo Park, New York.

• • • •

The property on which Buckingham Palace is located was once the site of a brothel.

• • • •

The chance of an expectant mother having quadruplets is 1 in 681,472.

F.A.O. as in the Schwarz toy store stands for Frederick August Otto.

• • • •

In the mid 1800's there were more buffalo than people in the U.S.

• • • •

Princeton University, in order to distinguish itself from the "yard" of Harvard, originated the term "campus".

• • • •

Twin towers: Michael and James Lanier, born November 27, 1969, are the world's tallest identical twins. Both stand 7'4".

• • • •

Blondes may not necessarily have more fun, but they do have more hair. A blonde has about 150,000 hairs in the scalp while a brunette has 100,000. Redheads have about 90,000 scalp hairs.

• • • •

Two words in the English language which have consecutive u's are residuum and vacuum. A word with three u's would be unusual.

• • • •

The largest organ on your body is the skin.

• • • •

Walt Disney's Goofy was originally called Dippy Dawg.

• • • •

A female mule is called a jenny; a male mule is called a jack. (The author of this book is not particularly proud of the latter.)

• • • •

74% of Americans keep their paper money in order of denomination in their bill fold.

• • • •

Rhode Island is so tiny—48 miles from north to south, 37 miles east to west—that you're never more than an hour away from any point within the state.

Chinese checkers originated in England.

Privia

The Pentagon uses an average of 666 rolls of toilet paper every day.

Australia, Great Britain, Greece and Switzerland are the only four nations which have competed in all of the modern Summer Olympic Games.

• • • •

George Carlin, Peter Jennings, Vidal Sassoon, John Chancellor, Harry Belafonte, Michael J. Fox, and Glen Campbell were all high school dropouts.

• • • •

Squirrels can climb faster than they can run.

• • • •

The United States flag, put on the moon on July 20, 1969, was made of metal to withstand rock and dust debris.

Marvin Hamlisch was the youngest person ever accepted to the Juilliard School of Music. He was 7.

• • • •

How many hours a day are your eyes closed? It depends of course on how long you sleep, but that isn't the only factor. Blinking causes each eye to be closed an additional half hour every day.

• • • •

Arlington National Cemetery is located on General Robert E. Lee's homestead.

• • • •

While you're reading this item, three more babies have been born into the world.

• • • •

The longest acronym in the English language is 26 letters: COMSUBCOMNELMCOMHEDSUPPACT. It stands for Commander, Subordinate Command, United States Naval Forces Eastern Atlantic and Mediterranean, Commander Headquarters Support Activities.

• • ••

Trivia Challenge #5

1. True or false? Literary genius Edgar Allan Poe was a crossword puzzle fanatic with a macabre sense of humor. His tombstone reads, "Edgar Allan Poe — six down."

2. Who is older, Donald Duck or Mickey Mouse?

3. Brandophiles are:
    a. Cowboys who hot-stamp cattle
    b. Shoppers who refuse to buy generic goods
    c. Collectors of cigar bands
    d. Marlon Brando groupies

4. Humans have to do it when they sneeze. Frogs have to do it in order to swallow. What is it?

5. Alaska and Hawaii became the 49th and 50th states back in 1959. Which was the 48th state?

6. What's the only way to tell a male penguin from a female? (Assuming you're not a penguin, that is.)

7. Which U.S. President was so long-winded in his inaugural, he was short-lived thereafter?

8. What's unique about the following sentence? Bores are people that say that people are bores.

9. Walt Disney World in Florida and Disneyland in California are both, coincidentally, located in counties of the same name. What is it?

10. Name the TV families that lived at:
    a. 704 Hauser Street
    b. 1313 Mockingbird Lane
    c. 39 Stone Canyon Way

Answers

1. *False. Poe was already six down when Arthur Wynne came across with the first crossword puzzle in America on December 21, 1913, in the "New York World".*

2. *Mickey, "born" in 1928, is six years older.*

3. *C. (And we're not just blowing smoke . . .)*

4. *Close their eyes.*

5. *Arizona, in 1912.*

6. *By autopsy.*

7. *William Henry Harrison, who, after speaking for two hours in freezing rain, died of pneumonia one month later.*

8. *It's a "pseudodrome" — a phrase in which the words read the same backwards and forwards.*

9. *Orange County.*

10. *The Bunkers, The Munsters and The Flintstones, respectively.*

It takes five seconds for the sound of thunder to travel a mile.

Privia

In 1878, Harley Procter got divine inspiration for the name "Ivory Soap" while he was sitting in church listening to a passage from the Bible about "ivory palaces".

• • • •

Superman's birthday is February 29.

• • • •

With all due respect to *Sesame Street*, the world's real Big Bird is the ostrich. The biggest of our fine feathered friends grows to an average height of 17 feet and weighs up to 340 pounds.

• • • •

On an average day, Americans drink a total of three million gallons of orange juice.

• • • •

How many feet does a centipede have? Depending on the species, anywhere from 28 to 354.

• • • •

An American survey showed that only 9% of the public could name the Chief Justice of the Supreme Court whereas 54% could identify the judge of *The People's Court*. How about you?

• • • •

There are about 12 times as many Irish eyes smiling in the U.S. as there are in Ireland.

Privia

Former Beatle George Harrison has a toilet seat lid that plays *Lucy in the Sky with Diamonds.*

• • • •

The one-millionth trademark from the U.S. Patent Office was granted to Sweet 'N Low.

• • • •

The White House was originally gray, but after the British torched it during the War of 1812, it was repainted white to hide the smoke stains.

• • • •

The $10,000 bill is limited to a circulation of 400.

• • • •

If you suffer from polydactylism, you have more than your fair share of fingers or toes.

• • • •

The Rolls Royce monogram was changed from red to black upon the death of Sir Henry Royce in 1933.

• • • •

You'll be happy to know that your Social Security number is and always will be unique to you. It will be retired after you die.

• • • •

Dogs bite 28 mail carriers in the U.S. every day.

Edgar Allan Poe was expelled from West Point in 1831 because he showed up at a parade in his birthday suit.

• • • •

The most common last-name initial in the U.S. is "S".

Privia

When Sir Winston Churchill lost his seat in Parliament, someone saw fit to cable this message to him: "What good is a W.C. without a seat?"

• • • •

Epee is the only four-letter word with three e's.

• • • •

Jacob German, a New York City cab driver, holds the distinction of being the first person arrested for speeding. He was cited on May 20, 1899 — for going 12 miles per hour.

• • • •

Parting Words

We leave you with a potty-pourri of last impressions from the famous, infamous and just plain funny.

First, a handful of self-written epitaphs, some of which obviously have not yet been etched in stone:

"Here stands Tony Randall. I am not going to take this lying down."

—Tony Randall

• • • •

"I told you I was ill."

—Spike Milligan

• • • •

"Keep the line moving."

—Jack Paar

• • • •

"If this is a joke — I don't get it."

—David Brenner

• • • •

Good Friend, for Jesus' sake forbeare
To dig the dust enclosed here.
Blessed be he that spares these stones,
And curst be he that moves my bones.
—William Shakespeare, 1616

• • • •

"Quoth the Raven Nevermore"
—Edgar Allan Poe, 1849

• • • •

Like the cover of an old book,
Its contents torn out,
And stripped of its lettering and gilding,
Lies here, Food for worms,
But the work shall not be wholly lost;
For it will, as he believed, Appear once more,
In a new and more perfect Edition
Corrected and Amended
By the Author.
—Benjamin Franklin, 1790

Tombstones provide survivors with some last laughs about the dearly departed as demonstrated by the following few:

In memory of Mrs. Alpha White
Weight 309 lbs.
Open wide, ye heavenly gates
—found in a Lee, Massachusetts, cemetery

• • • •

Here lies Ann Mann;
She lived an old maid and
She died an Old Mann.
—Bath Abbey, England

• • • •

Under the sod and under the trees
Lies the body of Solomon Pease.
He is not here, there's only the pod:
Pease shelled out and went to God.
—Barre, Vermont

• • • •

And now, some famous last words:

Ludwig van Beethoven, composer who had impaired hearing much of his life, died in 1827: "I shall hear in heaven."

William McKinley, 24th U.S. President, was assassinated in 1901. His last words: "We are all going, we are all going, we are all going . . . oh dear!"

• • • •

Douglas Fairbanks, Sr., actor, died in 1939: "I've never felt better."

• • • •

Sir Winston Churchill, British statesman who died in 1965: "Oh, I am so bored with it all."

• • • •

Leonardo da Vinci, artist and inventor who died in 1519: "I have offended God and mankind because my work did not reach the quality it should have."

• • • •

Henry Ward Beecher, Congregationalist preacher, died in 1887: "Now comes the mystery."

• • • •

Pablo Picasso, painter who died in 1973: "Drink to me."

General John Sedgwick, Union commander in the Civil War, was killed in a battle in 1864. He uttered these last words while looking over a parapet at the enemy lines: "They couldn't hit an elephant at this dist– –"

•   •   •   •

Rudolph Valentino, movie star who died in 1926: "Don't pull down the blinds! I feel fine. I want the sunlight to greet me."

•   •   •   •

William Somerset Maugham, author who died in 1965: "Dying is a very dull, dreary affair. And my advice to you is to have nothing whatever to do with it."

•   •   •   •

Edgar Allan Poe, writer; died in 1849: "Lord help my poor soul."

•   •   •   •

Finally, these last words come from German philosopher Karl Marx in 1883, when asked if he had one last message for the world: "Go on, get out! Last words are for fools who haven't said enough."